Painting
Glass

IN A WEEKEND

Stylish designs and practical projects

MOIRA NEAL

AND LYNDA HOWARTH

NH
NEW
HOLLAND

To Tony and Jim

This edition first published in 2002 by
New Holland Publishers (UK) Ltd
London • Cape Town • Sydney • Auckland
www.newhollandpublishers.com

Garfield House
86-88 Edgware Road
London W2 2EA
United Kingdom

80 McKenzie Street
Cape Town 8001
South Africa

Level 1, Unit 4, 14 Aquatic Drive
Frenchs Forest, NSW 2086
Australia

218 Lake Road
Northcote, Auckland
New Zealand

ISBN 1 85368 816 9 (pb)

Editor: Gillian Haslam
Designer: Peter Crump
Photographer: Shona Wood

Editorial Direction: Yvonne McFarlane

Reproduction by Modern Age Repro House Ltd, Hong Kong
Printed and bound in Malaysia by Times Offset (M) sdn. Bhd

Important
Every effort has been made to present clear and accurate
instructions. The author and publishers can accept no
liability for any injury, illness or damage which may
inadvertently be caused to the user while following them.

Front cover
The border design featured on the front cover requires some artistic
talent and familiarity both with the paint and the basic techniques.
Practise 'splaying' the paint with one brush stroke to achieve the fern
effect. The stems and ferns on the template on page 77 are merely
guidelines for the brush stroke to follow – it is the way the paint is
applied that gives the finished effect. Mix your colours and experiment
before you start by dipping your brush into lots of colours together to
get the mixed colour finish. Try to make the flowers 'flow' across the
glass so they look more natural.

Also shown on the front cover are two perfume bottles decorated with
gold paint (see page 48 for a similar project) and a coloured glass
with a gold rim (see page 32 for a similar project and remember to use
a non-toxic paint if decorating close to the lip line).

CONTENTS

INTRODUCTION

Decorating glassware has been a popular craft for centuries and indeed some of the glass in this book has been inspired by old Venetian work. Now that there are so many excellent products on the market, glass painting is enjoying an enormous revival and every craft magazine on the newsagents' shelves contains yet more ideas and designs.

We have inspired, supported, amused and entertained each other for almost twenty years. On many occasions our children have been reared in the inevitable chaos associated with combining our talents in creative ventures. We both became interested in glass painting when a new product, Porcelaine 150, became available which has very good dishwasher resistance and is safe to use with food — this idea really appealed and has revolutionised the craft. It means that as well as making purely decorative items or ones needing careful hand-washing, everyday glassware may be painted which will stand up to tough washing.

During the past few months we have been busy painting, stencilling, sponging, marbling and etching any and every glass item in our homes, our friends' and parents' homes. Our craving to embellish has included anything from humble jam jars and wine bottles to carafes and glasses, mirrors and even window panes ... nothing has escaped the Lynda and Moira treatment. It has led to our homes being filled with glasses no-one is allowed to drink from in case they dare drop them before this book is printed!

Trips for the weekly food shop have taken on a new appeal. Never mind what the product is, tastes like or costs — what will the bottle look like given a coat of paint? This has led to severe confusion. Just what IS that strange yellow stuff in that jam jar in the fridge? Is it mustard dressing, lemon and honey vinaigrette or custard? And how long does it keep for? If only we had labelled things before parting the mysterious contents from their beautiful containers!

And as for Jim, Lynda's husband — he became increasingly bewildered that the sponge cloth used for washing the dishes was getting smaller by the day (it was a truly marvellous discovery when we found just how good they are for sponging glassware)! All we can say is thank you Jim for putting up with us, our mess, our glass, our experiments and our masterpieces! It has certainly spared Tony, who, as anyone who has read *Dough Craft in a Weekend* will know, has a strong aversion to Moira and her mess!

We have had enormous fun putting together all the ideas in this book and we hope that you will be inspired by them. No particular artistic skill is required as we have described, step-by-step, how to arrive at the finished designs. We have provided templates and patterns where necessary but you will see from the gallery shots just how much stylish glassware can be made with just a few simple brushstrokes and dots of outliner.

Have fun!

Moira and Lynda... partners in design

GETTING STARTED

One of the greatest advantages of painting on glass is that the craft requires very little in the way of specialised tools or equipment – just a plentiful supply of new or old glassware which can be picked up for very little money. You will probably discover that much of the equipment listed below can be found around the home. This chapter explains the different paints and demonstrates the basic decorating techniques used in the projects that follow later in the book. Once you have mastered these, you will be able to create a wide range of effects and finishes and adapt them to make your own patterns.

SOURCING GLASSWARE

If, like us, you are delighted to have an excuse to go to a car boot fair or a jumble or garage sale, glass painting gives you the perfect reason! So much beautiful old glassware is available in an abundance of shapes and sizes at very reasonable prices. Even a batch of dissimilar glasses can be united into a set simply by painting them with the same colour or design motifs.

Look for unusual items such as goldfish bowls, old perfume bottles, engraved glasses, picture frames, clip frames, mirrors and vases.

Make sure you clean your glass very thoroughly before you begin painting. Really stubborn stains inside bottles may be removed with denture cleaner dissolved in hot water. Sticky labels can often be removed by rubbing with a drop of nail varnish remover on a pad of cotton wool.

EQUIPMENT AND MATERIALS

Your local hobby shop, paint outlet or mail order company will be able to supply the glass paints and other basic materials to get you started. Begin with just a few colours and add to them gradually as your skill and enthusiasm grow. The other equipment you will need to begin is listed in detail in the middle column of this page.

As soon as you have bought your glass paints you will be inspired to make a start. Do not be surprised if your first efforts look very amateurish as it can take a few projects to master this skill. It is therefore a good idea to start off with a really simple design on a jam jar in order to become familiar with the texture of the paint and its application.

It will not be long before you have exhausted your own supply of plain glass and will be requesting friends and relatives to collect empty containers for you too. Everyday packaging suddenly becomes remarkably interesting once the labels are removed and a little imagination is employed!

| Interesting jars, bottles and glassware |
| Good quality brushes, no 2 and 4 |
| Glass paints according to the project required. Some are solvent-based and suitable for decorative items. For more durability, choose oven-bake water-based paints |
| Outliner in a variety of colours |
| White spirit |
| Jam jar |
| Kitchen paper towels |
| Low-tack masking tape |
| Pencil |
| Scalpel with no 11 blade or craft knife |
| Tracing paper |
| Cocktail sticks (toothpicks) |
| Sponge or fur fabric |
| Cotton buds |
| Cellophane |
| Hairdryer |
| Apron |
| Newspaper, to protect your worksurface |
| Additional useful items for styling your finished work include raffia and florist's wire |

TIP

To keep the mess down, once you are ready to begin, protect your workspace with layers of old newspaper or an old tablecloth as some of the paints are solvent-based and may damage some surfaces.

If children are going help with the painting, make sure they are also well covered up.

SAFETY NOTES

There is no reason why children cannot enjoy the hobby of glass painting as well as adults. Make sure that they are supervised at all times and choose water-based paints for them to use. Store paints and brush cleaner in a cool place, well out of the reach of prying hands when not in use.

Always follow manufacturers' specific instructions regarding the baking process if it is required (see facing page for more details).

A collection of glassware ready for painting

GLASS PAINTING PRODUCTS

There are many paints available on the market for painting on glass. They tend to fall into several categories:

1 Water-based paints. These do not need baking and are ideal for items which will not require washing. These are perfect for children to use too.

2 Water-based paints. These need to be baked at 200°C/400°F/gas mark 6 for 30 minutes. Items using this paint are hand-washable. The colours are bright and dense and easy to apply.

3 Porcelaine 150, Pébéo's water-based paints. These are baked at 150°C/300°F/gas mark 2. These are completely safe when in contact with food and have good dishwasher resistance. These are ideal for tableware and glasses and we have used them extensively in this book. They are available in a huge range of colours, both transparent

and opaque, and once baked feel wonderfully smooth. Practice may be needed with these, as indeed with all paints, to achieve the density of cover required. It is often better to sponge on two light coats, allowing the first to dry before applying the second. There is a matt medium in the range which, if used alone, gives a wonderful, frosted effect. Used with the other colours in the range as instructed, it gives a matt finish without affecting the colour.

4 Pébéo's water-based gel paints. A new product on the market is a water-based gel which allows three-dimensional colour to be applied to glassware direct from the tube or with the aid of a palette knife. Glass nuggets, tiny mirrors and other items may then be embedded in the gel before it sets for an exotic effect. This enables you to imitate various blown glass effects, as well as creating stylish jewellery. Available in a range of colours, the gel liquifies when shaken or stirred so may also be applied with a brush.

5 Solvent-based paints. These tend to be the paints associated with the traditional stained glass look and are

mainly transparent and quick drying. Replace the tops to prevent evaporation. Brushes need to be cleaned using a compatible solvent, generally white spirit. These paints are flammable and should not be used near a naked flame nor should children use them unsupervised. Make sure your work area is well ventilated.

SAFETY NOTE

Please refer to manufacturer's specific user and safety instructions regarding all glass paints. As a general rule, never paint any surface which is to come into contact with food unless the paint is non-toxic (this is why we decorated the backs of the plates) and as an extra precaution, avoid the lip line on glasses which are going to be functional and not simply used as decorations.

OUTLINING

The outliners used in this book are water-based, although there are some which become permanent with baking. They can be difficult to control, so practise on jam jars or cellophane before embarking on the real thing.

Have a sheet of kitchen paper ready to catch any blobs of outliner from the tube which may appear as soon as the top is removed. Start by making a row of dots and you will soon realise how little pressure is required on the tube. Progress to circles, squares, triangles and lines ①, using the practice templates on page 76. You may find you get a halo effect at times — do not worry as this can be salvaged once the outliner has dried and can be eased back into place with the scalpel. A hairdryer is useful for speeding up the drying times of both outliners and paints but needs to be kept at least 15 cm (6 in) away from the surface to avoid damage.

USING THE GLASS PAINTS

Within about five minutes the outliner will be dry enough to apply the paint. A soft brush is essential for smooth application of the paints ①. Try filling in some of the shapes you have made with the outliners. Apply the paint with even strokes. Keep a cotton bud nearby to correct any errors and a small jar of water or solvent for brush cleaning.

SPONGING

Sponging gives a soft, delicate effect and is a very quick and easy way to apply glass paints.

Tip a few drops of the paint into a saucer (covered with cling film to reduce the cleaning up). Gently dip in your sponge pad and wipe any excess off against the edge of the dish and then test the effect on a piece of cellophane or an old jam jar before starting on your project.

One colour can be used on its own to produce a graded effect just by applying more paint onto the lowest part of the item, reducing the pressure and contact as you move up ②. A graduated effect is achieved by using several colours in succession, allowing each one to merge into the next ③.

TIP

Thin sponge dishcloths are ideal for glass painting as they can be cut up into small pieces and discarded after use. Fine fur fabric also produces an even sponged finish but the rough edges should be folded in before use to prevent any fibres migrating onto the surface of the glass.

SPONGE DOT APPLICATORS

A really simple way to apply uniform dots to a project is to make your own applicators. Peel a foam dishcloth into two and then cut it into 2 cm (¾ in) squares. Bind each one over the end of a cocktail stick or toothpick using fuse wire. Make several as you will find them a useful addition to your equipment kit!

STENCILLING

This is a good way to decorate glassware with a regular repeat pattern. It is particularly useful if you intend to sell your finished items as it is very quick to do once the initial stencil cutting has been done.

To make your stencils, photocopy the required template (see page 77), use adhesive mount to attach it to the card you are using and allow the glue to dry for about ten minutes before attempting to cut it. Protect your worksurface with a cutting mat, cork mat or a thick layer of newspaper before you start. Use a metal ruler as a guide for cutting straight lines ①. Avoid trying to cut around angular designs in one go; instead, make several shorter cuts ②.

It is worth taking care in order to get good, professional results and the initial investment in a craft knife or scalpel and plenty of spare blades is worthwhile. For one-off stencils to decorate flat surfaces, thin card is ideal or even a good quality paper. If you are using your stencil on a curved surface, you may need to use either thin paper or specialist adhesive stencilling film which moulds more easily to the contours of the glass.

USING STENCILS

Lightly spray the back of the stencil with aerosol glue and press it onto the object to be decorated. On cylindrical items you may also need to secure the stencil with a couple of rubber bands.

③ Pour a little glass paint into a saucer and use either a piece of old reinforcements or indeed any shape you care to cut out of paper.

Use aerosol adhesive mount to apply your own shapes to the glass. Masking tape, torn strips of newspaper and very thin tape available from art shops can also be used. Squares, oblongs, stripes of varying widths and harlequin designs are all possible this way, producing very effective results ①, ②.

It is so easy to produce fabulous glassware with minimal artistic ability using these ideas. If you wish, the masked off area can later be embellished with outliner to add a relief pattern, such as the veining on a leaf. This method can also be used to add a regular pattern, for example to the outer edge of a plate.

Simple, Shaker-style stencil, ideal for beginners

sponge or fur fabric to apply the paint. It is always worth experimenting at this stage and we found that fur fabric works wonderfully well for a fine, even texture. Sponge will give a rougher, less even texture which is more suitable for rustic style projects ④.

MASKING AND REVERSE STENCILLING

Many different objects can be used to mask out clear areas on the glass before you decorate with sponging or marbling. Stick on shapes like stars, hearts, flowers, initials, ring

ETCHING

This is a very good way to add embellishment without having to use another colour. It is perfect for adding details like feathers, scales on fish, eyes and so on as well as creating abstract designs on a sponged surface. You will need to etch the design as soon as the paint has been applied and there are several ways of doing it. Use a cocktail stick or toothpick for very fine designs or for details on tiny items. A typist's 'pencil' type of rubber is ideal for chunkier etching and may be sharpened with a knife or pencil sharpener depending on the effect required ①. Knitting needles work well too.

MARBLING

A wonderful range of patterns may be produced using this technique which involves floating coloured solvent-based glass paints on a suitable medium. We have kept the procedure simple and have avoided the use of specialist marbling mediums in preference for water and wallpaper paste. You will need to use a bowl larger than the size of the item to be marbled and cover the worksurface with plenty of paper before you begin.

Two of the projects in this book have marbling as one of the stages of producing the final item. Refer to pages 22 and 58 for fuller instructions.

Sponged and etched snowflake plate

An exotic effect created by marbling a simple piece of glass

TRANSFERRING DESIGNS

The easiest way to transfer a design onto glass is to trace it. Tape the design to the inside or back of the object to hold it firmly against the glass. If the surface is curved, make many small vertical slits to enable the pattern to conform to the glass. Trace over the pattern with outliner.

NARROW NECKED BOTTLES

It is impossible to tape the design to the inside of narrow necked bottles but there is a simple solution. Make sure the bottle is dry inside and then, on a piece of paper, cut out the design to the height of the bottle. Roll up the paper, push it into the bottle, then pour in pasta or lentils right up to the top and the design is perfectly anchored! ①

❷

❶

REVERSE PAINTING TECHNIQUE

This is a very handy way to decorate the back of a glass plate so that the cutting surface will not become

damaged when the plate is used. It is also useful if you wish to use paints which are not safe when in contact with food. A little planning is needed before you begin because the details, normally left until last, must be painted on first. Just think in reverse and remember to reverse any text too!

EMBELLISHMENTS

The addition of those lovely shiny glass nuggets available in a myriad of colours gives a very splendid finish to an otherwise ordinary item. Tiny rhinestones and sequins may be used too and they are available from craft shops or mail order companies ②.

Apply them to your glassware before the paint using a specialist glass glue to

These iridescent nuggets inspired this floral design

Matt medium was applied over a star stencil for this subtle effect

ensure good adhesion. If you are giving a filled, decorated bottle to a friend as a present, spend some time adding a label, a pretty stopper or sealing wax. See our gallery pages for more ideas. Remember, a beautifully presented item will quickly lead to orders if you want to sell your glassware.

INSPIRATION FOR DESIGNS

Wrapping paper, gift cards, colouring books, curtain fabrics, flower and bulb catalogues are good sources of inspiration. Do remember, however, that you may not sell any work using other people's designs.

For a baby gift you could use the nursery wallpaper design to inspire the edge of a mirror or picture frame. Glasses, jugs and carafes decorated to match existing crockery or table linen make excellent gifts for adults and may be themed to celebrate a special occasion, such as a milestone birthday or anniversary.

If you enjoy museums, why not visit one and get inspiration from old

Venetian glassware? We found some fascinating pieces where much of the design is made up of dots and swirls — very easy to reproduce as you will see from our Historical Gallery on page 30.

This design was adapted from traditional East European glassware

PROJECTS AND GALLERIES
FOR PAINTING GLASS

GOLDFISH PLATE

A shoal of golden fish swim around this plate which is both practical and attractive. You could use it to brighten up your bathroom, and could decorate other items such as a soap dish or toothbrush mug to match. As the plate is decorated on the underside, it may be used for serving food.

1 Wash the plate in hot soapy water and dry carefully. Start by sponging the edge of the plate on the underside with the gold paint, applying it densely around the outside. Allow the paint to look feathery on the inner edge. Use the paper towel and white spirit to clean any paint from the front of the plate.

YOU WILL NEED

A glass plate
Solvent-based glass paints in gold and white
Fine sponge or fur fabric
White spirit
Kitchen paper towels
No 2 paintbrush
Cellophane to practise on
Kitchen paper towels
Fish and surf templates (page 70)
Sticky tape
Paper
Pen
Scissors
Cocktail stick (toothpick)
Aerosol spray mount
Saucer covered with cling film

VARIATIONS

This plate could be painted using oven-bake paints if you want to preserve the pattern during frequent use. It seems a pity to hide it away in a cupboard when not in use, so why not store it on a plate display stand?

2 Copy the large fish template and tape it to the inside of the plate, positioning it centrally. Working on the back of the plate, paint the fish gold, but do not apply the markings at this stage.

3 Remove the template and use it as a guide to etch in the details of the scales and gills using the cocktail stick. Keep the tip clean with the paper towel.

4 Paint the shoal of tiny goldfish next. This time have a practise run on cellophane first as it is easier to copy the tiny shapes we have given you. Use the cocktail stick to etch in the details after every third or fourth fish. For a bit of fun, paint one little fish swimming the wrong way! Allow the plate to dry for about an hour while you make the surf template for the next stage.

5 Draw around the plate onto a piece of paper. Cut out the circle and then fold it in half four times to make 16 equal sections. Open it out flat and mark 1 cm (½ in) in from the edge all the way round. Trace the surf template onto each marked section. Pour some of the white paint onto the saucer, dip the sponge into it and wipe the excess off on the edge. Sponge the surf design all around the plate. Remove the template and quickly soften the edges of the wave design by carefully sponging over it. Turn the plate over every now and then to check what it looks like from the front. Leave the plate upside down to dry for 24 hours before use.

OLIVE OIL BOTTLES

This project would make an ideal present. After painting the the olives and leaves on the glass, we filled the bottles with finest quality olive oil and attached a small pastry brush by drilling through the handle and attaching a length of wire. Choose a brush which is slightly shorter than the bottle.

1 First, wash and dry the bottle thoroughly inside and out. Trace or photocopy the template and cut it out close to the edge of the design. Tape a piece of ribbon or string to the top for easy removal from narrow necked bottles. Push the template into the bottle. Fill the bottle with pasta to anchor the paper in place and then stopper it firmly.

YOU WILL NEED

A tall bottle (ours is 27 cm (11 in) tall) with a cork stopper	Solvent-based glass paints in brown, emerald green, yellow, red and blue
Template (page 70)	Saucer covered with cling film for mixing colours
Paper	White spirit
Pen	Cocktail stick (toothpick)
Scissors	Kitchen paper towel
Sticky tape	Wooden pastry brush (optional)
Ribbon or string	Drill (optional)
Pasta, baking beans or similar	Florist's wire (optional)
No 2 paintbrush	

VARIATIONS

This bottle would make a lovely gift for anyone to display in their kitchen. Use this idea for salad dressings too. Artistically minded people will have fun decorating bottles of flavoured oil or vinegar with sprays of chillies or a variety of herbs.

2 Start by painting the olive branches using the brown paint darkened with a little blue if necessary. You may find it easier to rest your hand on something of similar height (we found a paper towel roll works very well as a cushion to steady the wrist).

3 You need to mix emerald green with a little brown and yellow to achieve the leaf shade we have used. Test the colour on cellophane but remember it does not have to be botanically correct! Paint in the leaves using the illustration as a guide. Use the white spirit to keep your brush clean and to remove mistakes.

4 Etch in the details of the leaves using a cocktail stick. It is best to do this as soon as possible before the paint has time to dry. This technique really does bring the leaves to life. Alternatively, paint in the veins using a darker shade of green.

5 Finally, paint in the olives using a mixture of red, blue and brown. If you are happy with your work, allow it to dry thoroughly. If not, remove it and start again! To give the bottle a rustic appearance, add a hook made from wire which is then twisted around the neck of the bottle. Fill the bottle with extra virgin olive oil and then firmly wire the cork stopper in place.

FAUX TORTOISESHELL PLATE

This plate was inspired by the fascinating shapes and colours of natural tortoiseshell. Why not do as we have and create a complete set of matching glassware using different sized bottles and pots? A combination of painting and marbling was used and we can guarantee that you will end up with a totally unique piece each time!

1 Wash and dry the plate before you begin in order to remove any grease. Paint the back of the plate with the yellow paint using long brushstrokes. Do not try to get this too even as imperfections will add to the natural look of the plate. Leave it to dry or speed up the process with a hairdryer.

YOU WILL NEED

Glass plate

Plenty of paper to protect your worksurface

Solvent-based glass paints such as Vitrail in yellow, brown and burnt umber

No 4 (or larger) paintbrush

Hairdryer (optional)

Large bowl of cold water at least 7 cm (3 in) wider than the plate

Pipettes

Cocktail sticks (toothpicks)

White spirit

Polyurethane varnish (optional)

VARIATIONS

Why stick to traditional tortoiseshell colours? As long as the base colour is pale and will tone with the two marbled coats, all kinds of variations are possible. It is worth experimenting on cellophane before you reach a decision as it is much simpler to throw it out than it is to clean a plate!

2 Fill the bowl with water and then fill the pipettes with both the brown paints. Quickly drop the paint on the surface of the water and allow the drops to merge slightly. Position the plate over the marbled surface and 'roll' the plate away from you picking up the marbled pattern on the back of the plate (see step 4 below). Place the plate upside down to dry.

3 For the second marbling, a more spattered effect is achieved by squirting the paints over the water so that it breaks up into smaller drops. Any unsightly blobs may be carefully removed using a cocktail stick to roll the paint off the surface of the water.

4 Again, lower the plate onto the marbled surface as indicated in step 2, above. Leave the plate upside down to dry once more. You can use a hairdryer to speed up the drying process, if you wish.

5 Touch up any imperfections using a fine brush and the yellow basecoat and leave to dry for at least 24 hours before use. For extra scratch resistance, the back may be painted with two coats of polyurethane varnish.

YELLOW GALLERY

'Volcano' oil burner
This has been etched and over-painted.

Orange slices jar
A citrus effect was achieved by applying the paint with a very small brush and fine brushstrokes.

Tall yellow bottle
This elegant bottle has been stencil-frosted for a pretty finish.

Shallow yellow platter
A very simple gold border was painted around this dish for a striking effect.

Cup and saucer
Luscious apricots were painted on this cup using opaque glass paints.

Shaped glasses
One glass has been painted with simple bands of yellow and gold and the other given an iridescent effect by being lightly sponged first with gold and then with a clear yellow. A simple band of gold dots was added later.

1940s' style glass dessert dish
Bottom: The embossed lines on this dish made it very simple to decorate with yellows, orange and gold.

Perfume bottle
Matt medium was used on this little bottle first and then the yellow paint applied, making the glass appear transparent again.

Hexagonal jar
Bottom: Low-tack tape was used to mask off alternate facets before marbling with yellow, orange and gold. Gold outliner dots were added later.

Tall, pale yellow glass
The bowl of this glass was made from pale lemon glass but a deeper colour was overlaid using clear yellow paint.

Copper glass
This glass was frosted with matt medium first before a coat of copper was sponged over the bottom section.

Stripy frosted glass
Strips of paper were used to mask off areas and matt medium then sponged on to give a frosted look.

MILLEFIORI LANTERN

This lantern was inspired by the wonderful range of colours found in millefiori beads. It is surprisingly easy to reproduce the design but can only be successfully done on a flat surface. As the panels of this lantern are removable, it is ideal for decorating in this way and candlelight enhances the rich colours.

1 Clean the panels of glass using glass cleaner, being very careful of the sharp edges. (Wear the leather gloves for protection.) Lay your glass onto a sheet of paper and draw round it and then use small coins as templates as shown. If you prefer, use the template on page 71.

YOU WILL NEED

Lantern
Glass cleaner
Old leather gloves for handling the glass
Paper
Pencil
Small coins or template (page 71)
Oven-bake outliners (we used Porcelaine 150) in green, blue, red, yellow and orange
Kitchen paper towels
Cocktail stick (tooth pick)
Domestic oven

— VARIATIONS —

Faceted bottles and jam jars may be decorated using this method but make sure that your chosen item is kept completely level at all times until baked.

2 Lay the panel of glass onto the pattern and remove the lids from all the tubes of outliners before you begin. It is best to work on just three circles at a time and vary the colour combinations using an equal amount of colour overall. Begin with the red. The fluid nature of the outliners make them ideal for this project.

3 Continue to add more colours in circles and dots in an effort to achieve a star or floral effect. Note how well the colours look juxtaposed to the nearest colour in the rainbow, i.e. red, orange, yellow, green and blue. This stops complementary colours (e.g. orange and blue) merging and becoming sludgy within each 'bead'. Aim to use all the colours on each one and do not worry if your work looks blobby at this stage.

4 Once you have completed three of the 'beads', use the cocktail stick to start the feathering. Drag the colours in and out all the way round each one to create a spider's web effect and encourage the colours to blend and bleed into one another.

5 Continue to work down the panel of glass towards yourself to avoid smudging your work. The paint looks very dense and opaque at this stage until it is thoroughly dry. When you have finished the panel, set it aside and start the next one. Note how all the colours continue to bleed into each other. This will continue to happen as the panels are left to dry flat for at least the next 24 hours. Bake following the manufacturer's instructions. Allow to cool and then fill in the spaces with solvent-based glass paint if you wish. Leave to dry thoroughly before reassembling the lantern.

RUBY AND GOLD SUNDAE DISHES

The inspiration for this design comes from Middle Eastern tea glasses and if you are able to find any plain glasses, the design may be adapted to suit them.
If you are feeling adventurous, why not make a complete dinner service using this design?

1 Wash the glassware in hot soapy water, rinse and dry thoroughly. Cover your work area with paper before you begin. Use the rubber bands to mask off a parallel strip around the dish. The width may be varied depending on the size of your dish, but be sure to make them all equidistant.

YOU WILL NEED

Set of sundae dishes

Rubber bands 5 mm (¼ in) wide

Solvent-based glass paints such as
Vitrail in ruby and gold

No 2 paintbrush

White spirit for brush cleaning

Kitchen paper towels

Template (page 70)

Scalpel

Cellophane for practise runs

— VARIATIONS —

The dishes could each be painted in a different colour as long as each is strong enough to contrast with the gold. Practise first before going on to the real thing. The central band would make an attractive decoration on wine glasses too.

2 Fill the masked off area with the ruby paint, keeping the bowl clear of the work top to avoid smudging. Keep a paper towel to hand for brush cleaning before moving on to the next step.

3 The narrow gold bands are added next, along with the wavy gold line which forms the basis for the leaf and tendril design. Have a practise run on cellophane first using the template (see page 70) as a guide.

4 Once you are confident painting the leaf and tendril design, paint them on the bowls. If your artistic ability is not up to it, try painting little groups of three dots or simple tendrils instead.

5 Finally, work on the saucers. The leaf design is echoed around the edge in gold, followed by groups of three red dots in between.

HISTORICAL GALLERY

Spotted 1950s' style glass
Bottom: Use a fine brush to apply spots in a variety of colours.

Miniature perfume bottles
These little bottles are surprisingly cheap to buy and very quickly decorated with simple brushstrokes and outliner.

Old jam pot
The engraved design on this delightful old jam pot has been highlighted with gold, with fuschias delicately painted around the top.

Hexagonal jar
Bottom: Simple brushstrokes were used for the flowers and gold and white leaf shapes decorate the edges.

Venetian-style bottle
The simple brushstrokes on the edges of this bottle were inspired by old Venetian glassware. The lady was painted first with an opaque white and then the green and red clear paints applied on top.

Art Deco bottle
Simple lines and clean colours inspired by the Art Deco movement.

Champagne glass

Bottom: Red and green were drizzled down this old fashioned champagne glass and dots of colour added too.

Heraldic goblet

This is a good example of allowing the shape of the glass dictate the style of the embellishment. Here, the design has been added in black, white and gold.

Thistle glass

Bottom: This engraved bargain buy has been transformed with the use of colour.

Recycled perfume bottle

This beautiful lady in her crinoline dress is definitely for the more artistic reader!

Hexagonal boxes

Simple Art Nouveau motifs have been applied in gold and black.

ANTIQUED ETRUSCAN-STYLE VASE

The little stoppered jug used for this project started life filled with salad dressing which has now become one of the anonymous substances in the fridge! The idea can be adapted to any bottle or jug you can find either hiding at the back of your cupboard or on your next trip to the supermarket. Several pieces may be decorated in a similar way to make an interesting and original display.

1 Sponge the top half of the vase with the green paint allowing it to fade around the middle. The sponging can look quite rough as you are aiming for an aged look. Leave for a few minutes to dry between this and the next three steps.

4 Highlight the edges of the vase with the gold, including the rim and handle. The idea is to make the worn surfaces look metallic.

2 Using the blue paint, sponge from the bottom upwards and over the first coat. Allow the paint to fade out as you work upwards.

3 Antique over the base of the jug with the pewter, adding light touches of the metallic colour to the neck of the jug and the handle. Again, precision is unimportant as a rough look is more authentic.

5 Paint swirls of matt medium at random on the vase. The paint looks milky when it is applied but dries to a very subtle finish.

6 Echo the swirls using the pewter outliner. This dries to give an extra dimension to the vase. Leave the vase to dry for 24 hours before baking following manufacturer's instructions.

VARIATIONS

Try making a collection of glassware using this technique. Similar glassware is readily available and very quick to decorate in this way and several pieces could be painted at the same time.

FIFTIES STYLE CARAFE AND TUMBLERS

This really is a 20-minute project! It is brilliantly easy to do and as the shapes are so simple, they require no artistic ability – if you can write, you can reproduce them once you have mastered using the paints.

1 Copy the template on page 71 and lay the cellophane over it in order to have a practice run if you are not sufficiently confident to start straight onto the glassware. Keep a sheet of paper towel to hand and use it to keep the nozzle clean before drawing each motif. Apply the paints sparingly as they will spread slightly over the next ten minutes.

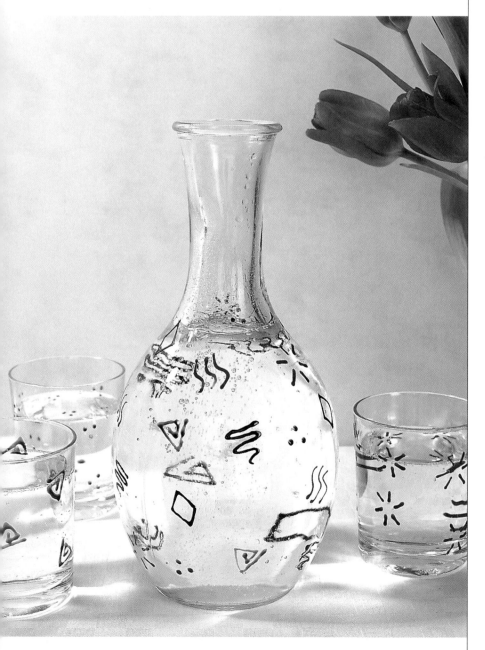

YOU WILL NEED

Carafe and six tumblers
Patterns (page 71)
Cellophane to practise on
Oven-bake outliners, such as Porcelaine 150, in green, magenta and black
Kitchen paper towels
Scalpel or craft knife
Domestic oven

— VARIATIONS —
Why not decorate the backs of glass plates and bowls to make a complete table setting?

2 Once you are ready to start on the glasses, wash them with hot, soapy water. The black squiggles are fun to do and it is best to do these freehand in order to get a flowing line. The black diamond design is easiest to work in two stages, working from the top to the bottom of one side and then the next.

3 Magenta sunbursts are worked from the outside inwards, making up the six spokes. The second magenta design of three wavy lines is then worked on the next glass.

4 The green triangular design is worked next and then the green dot design. Finally, transfer all the designs to the carafe, starting with the black, followed by the magenta and then the green. The groups of three dots can be added last of all as they are small and make good 'fillers'.

5 Leave all the glassware to dry for 24 hours and then use the scalpel to ease any stray outliner gently into place before baking following the manufacturer's instructions. Wash the glassware before use.

STAINED GLASS MIRROR

The colour selection of red, blue and green has made this simple mirror look quite exotic! The outline shapes could also be used as a solid design to decorate a wine bottle or jam jars with great success. It is easy enough for children to be able to imitate as long as they are carefully supervised, and a myriad of effects can be obtained depending on the colour selection used and the size of each shape.

1 Use glass cleaner to remove all traces of grease from the mirror before you begin. Cut the carbon paper to the size of the mirror and lay it face down onto it. Make a copy of the template, enlarging or reducing it as required and lay it over the carbon. Tape it in place. Use the coloured pencil to copy the outline onto the mirror so that you can see what you have already traced.

YOU WILL NEED

Mirror 23 x 18 cm (9 x 7 in)
Glass cleaner
Carbon paper
Scissors
Template (page 72)
Sticky tape
Sharp coloured pencil
Paper for protecting your work top
Solvent-based paints such as Vitrail in ruby red, blue and green
No 2 brush
White spirit for brush cleaning
Hairdryer (optional)
Lead effect outliner
Kitchen paper towels
Scalpel

TIP

The beauty of this project is that precision is unimportant so do not worry too much when you are copying the outlines! You may want to have more or less of the mirror showing than we have and it is easy to adjust this in step 1 by altering the size of the template using a photocopier.

2 Now the fun begins. Load the paintbrush with red paint and allow it to flow onto the mirror. Apply the paint quite thickly to produce a rich colourful effect. Paint about a quarter of the shapes this way. Clean the brush with the white spirit and allow the red areas to dry before using the next colour. This may be speeded up with the use of a hairdryer if you wish.

3 Apply the green to a further quarter of the shapes. It does not matter if the edges of your painted areas are uneven as the outliner will hide a multitude of sins!

4 Finally, use blue glass paint to fill in all but a quarter of the shapes. These remaining plain mirrored spaces can be embellished with the addition of rhinestones, glass nuggets or sequins, securing them in place with glass glue, or left plain as we have done.

5 Now use the outliner to trace over the pencil line in the mirror. Apply even pressure to the tube and have a paper towel to hand to keep the nozzle clean Finally, edge the mirror with the outliner to give a finished look. Allow the mirror to dry for about 24 hours before use, and polish off any fingerprints.

TASSELLED CHAMPAGNE GLASSES

Here is an imaginative idea to transform a set of champagne glasses into unique and expensive-looking tableware. As just one colour is used, there is little financial outlay and the results are stunning.

1 Wash the glasses in warm soapy water or clean them with spirit. Start by cutting a piece of paper about 2 cm (¾ in) wide and long enough to fit around the top of the glass and, if necessary, use a pencil to mark the cutting line. This is the template which will determine the height of the tassels but you can adjust it if you wish provided you keep the painted design clear of the lip line of the glass.

YOU WILL NEED

Champagne flutes
White spirit or warm soapy water
Paper
Pencil
Ruler
Scissors
Elastic band
Tassel and rope template (page 71)
Tube of gold Porcelaine 150 outliner
Kitchen paper towels
Domestic oven
Empty jam jars or cellophane (optional)

TIP

Before you begin you may like to experiment with the flow of the paint by testing it on a jam jar or cellophane first. As it is water-based it is easy to wipe off and start again and again until you are proficient. It is a good idea to keep the paper towels at hand to blot the nozzle before each attempt. You will find that the paint tends to spread slightly over the next ten minutes so it is best to avoid applying it too thickly.

2 Fold the paper into five, open it out and then secure it around the glass using an elastic band as shown. This is a quick and easy way to space the tassels evenly as each fold indicates the position of a tassel.

3 Use the glass paint to make five tiny dots around the glass to mark the position of the tassels as shown. Remove the paper and repeat on each glass.

4 Cut the template to fit inside the glass and hold it in place while tracing off the tassel with the gold outliner. (Remember to clean the nozzle with a paper towel before starting each one.) Move the template around and paint all five tassels.

5 Finally, link each tassel with the rope motif. Leave in a safe place for 24 hours to dry and then bake following manufacturer's instructions.

VARIATIONS

This design is equally suited to embellish a straight-sided jug and matching tumblers. As the design is so quick and simple to do, it could be used to decorate a large number of glasses for a special celebration. Why not use silver outliner for a 25th wedding anniversary for example?

BLUE, GOLD AND SILVER GALLERY

Tiny storage jar
Below: This little jar has been decorated with a variety of shells and a star fish and is an ideal container for beads.

Heart
Bottom: These little hanging plastic hearts were decorated using silver and gold outliners.

Snowflake plate
The silver edge was sponged first, followed by the blue. A typist's rubber was used to etch the snowflake shapes.

Old-fashioned sweet jar
This bottle was first sponged with white over the top part of the bottle and then, once dry, blue was sponged up from the bottom giving this wintry effect. Snowflakes were added using outliner.

Simple spiral designed glass
This delightful old glass has been brought right up to date with the simple addition of gold and blue banding.

Triangular blue bottle
Right: There is so much interestingly shaped and coloured glassware on the market now which can be decorated with opaque colours.

Tiny perfume bottles
Tiny hearts and a cherub have been painted on these little bottles using a fine brush and gold paint.

Frosted glass bottle

Bottom: This bottle started life filled with salad dressing! It was too pretty to throw away and has been transformed by being sponged with blue and silver and then decorated with silver snowflakes.

Marbled plate, bottle and jar

Blue, white and gold paints were floated on water and gently swirled to create these marbled patterns.

Storage jar

Here is a simple way to brighten up plain storage jars using deliberately uneven brush marks based on squares.

Wheat vase

Twenty minutes is all you need to add this simple wheat design in gold.

Small storage jar

Above: Use simple flowers, dots and scrolls to make this storage jar suitable for a bedroom or bathroom.

SUNFLOWER PLATE

This moulded plate lends itself to being painted as a sunflower. If you are unable to buy a similar one, the design could be applied to the back of a plain plate if you make a simple template first by folding a circle of paper into equal segments. Draw a circle for the centre of the flower and then stick the template onto the inside of the plate before you begin.

1 Lightly brush the petals and centre of the design with the gold. Use it sparingly so that the other colours, to be applied later, will shine through. Set aside to dry.

YOU WILL NEED

Glass plate — ours is 27 cm (10½ in)

Oven-bake paints such as Porcelaine 150 in gold, two shades of yellow, orange, black and brown

Cellophane

No 2 brush

Water

Domestic oven

2 It is time to experiment now while the gold paint dries. Use a piece of cellophane to work out the colour density you want to achieve before working on the plate. Use delicate brush strokes.

3 Use the palest shade of yellow first and brush it evenly, following the direction of the petals. Work the second yellow over it, working about two-thirds of the way up the petals so that the outer edges are paler.

4 Use the orange to darken from the centre of each petal to about half way down, using the brush almost dry to give a light, feathery look.

5 The centre of the sunflower is stippled using a mixture of brown, black and orange to give the appearance of seeds. Leave the plate to dry for 24 hours before baking according to the manufacturer's instructions. It may then be used and washed frequently without damage.

STARRY OIL BURNER

These beautiful, simple glass burners are perfect for decorating with glass paints and can be painted, etched or sponged to suit any occasion. They are available in several different shapes and sizes and are economic to run. No more dripping candle wax! Make sure you use oven-bake paints to prevent any lamp oil coming into contact with the surface and dissolving your creation.

1 Remove the wick and holder from the burner and plug the hole with adhesive putty. Wash the burner in hot, soapy water and dry thoroughly. Sponge the matt medium over the entire surface. Put some of the matt medium on the jam jar too as it will be useful in step 5. The paint looks transparent when it is first applied but it dries quickly. When dry, apply a second coat. A hairdryer will speed up the process.

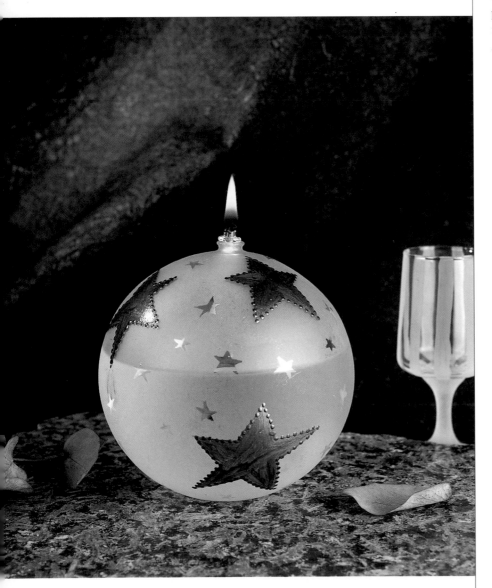

YOU WILL NEED

Round glass oil burner

Jam jar

Re-usable adhesive putty

Small piece of sponge

Oven-bake paints such Porcelaine 150 in pewter and matt medium

Porcelaine 150 pewter outliner

No 2 paintbrush

Water

Hairdryer (optional)

Large and small star templates (page 73)

Metal ruler

Scalpel with a 11 blade

Cutting mat

Pencil

Paper towels

Domestic oven

SAFETY NOTE

Always follow the manufacturer's instructions supplied with the lamp and never leave it unattended at any time, particularly if you have children or cats in the house.

2 Cut out the star templates using a metal ruler, cutting mat and scalpel. (Refer to the techniques section.) Use the pencil to draw the star outline onto the globe using the photograph as a guide for the spacing. Keep the motifs equidistant.

3 Paint the marked stars using the pewter paint. The matt base coat is a wonderful surface to paint over. For a really good cover, a second coat is needed.

4 Use the outliner to make rows of tiny dots round each star. Be careful to use the outliner sparingly as it continues to spread. Allow the globe to dry thoroughly before moving on to the next step.

5 The tiny stars are etched out using the scalpel and the template pattern provided. It is a good idea to practise on the jam jar first before starting on the real thing. Leave the globe to dry for 24 hours before baking following manufacturer's instructions. Once the globe is completely cool, fill it with lamp oil using a tiny funnel to avoid any getting onto the matt surface. Replace the wick in the bottle and light.

VARIATIONS

Use different coloured lamp oils to make the burner look festive or spring-like. It will look wonderful as a table decoration surrounded with ivy but make sure leaves are kept well away from the flame.

BLACK, SILVER AND GOLD GALLERY

Etched cork-stoppered jar
Bottom: This jar was frosted with matt medium with the design etched out afterwards.

Oak and acorn glass
Bottom: This design was stencilled on and the detail etched out with a cocktail stick.

Jug
Bottom: As simple as ABC! Letters were drawn on the jug and black dots added around the top.

Black plate
These stunning white brushstrokes look very oriental but are, in fact, simple random strokes.

Cocktail glass
Two coats of gold on the outside of this glass were followed by random black spots for a stylish finish.

Marbled plate
Here black, white and gold paints were floated on water and the design picked up on the back of the plate.

Frosted carafe
Oak leaves have been stencilled on this carafe using matt medium.

Art Deco jar

Bottom: This jar has been decorated very simply with stylised deer.

Glasses

Below: It is so easy to unite several dissimilar glasses like these with a common colour scheme. Black, gold and white paints and outliners were used to apply the designs.

Christmas bauble

Not even the humble bauble can escape decoration! This one was patterned with outliner.

Art Deco perfume bottle

Centre: This bottle was sponged with silver and gold before the stylised design was added in black.

Black and white dappled plate

Blobs of black and white paint were dropped onto the back of the plate and then spread and etched with a cocktail stick.

Perfume bottle

Bottom: This bottle embellished with trefoils was decorated in the same way as the project on page 48.

Gold and black glass

This glass was made in the same way as the set of decorated glasses with bands on page 28.

PERFUME BOTTLE

Have you ever thought what a pity it is to throw out your empty perfume bottles, especially when they are often such lovely shapes? Here is the answer. The design can be applied to any size or shape of bottle and a group of dissimilar bottles can be united in this way to make an attractive collection for the bedroom or bathroom.

1 Wash and dry the bottle thoroughly before you begin. Cover the entire surface by sponging it with the pewter paint. Apply two or three light coats, allowing the paint to dry between coats. In this way you will build up a really deep, lustrous surface. Allow to dry for 24 hours and bake following manufacturer's instructions. This will make a much better surface to work on and mistakes can be easily removed.

YOU WILL NEED

Small decorative bottle or empty perfume bottle

Oven-bake glass paints such as Porcelaine 150 in pewter, black and ivory

Fine sponge

Trefoil pattern (page 72)

Cellophane for practice runs

No 2 paintbrush

Water

Kitchen paper towels

Domestic oven

2 It is a good idea at this stage to have a practice run at painting the trefoils. To copy the pattern, lay cellophane over the template and paint as many as you need using one colour until you feel sufficiently confident to paint them freehand.

3 Check the spacing of the trefoils by laying the cellophane over your chosen bottle. This will give you an idea of how and where to place the shapes.

4 Now you are ready to start on the bottle. Paint all the ivory shapes in first, remembering to leave room for the other two colours.

5 Paint the black trefoils next and then fill in the gaps with a silvery mix of black and pewter. Leave to dry for a further 24 hours and bake again.

DECORATED WINE GLASSES

Here is a really clever way to decorate glasses and a matching carafe simply with the help of a few rubber bands. Use this technique to mask off sections which are then sponged in one colour. Neat rows of dots add a finishing touch. The perfect project for the non-artistic!

1 Wash all the items in hot soapy water and dry thoroughly. Place a rubber band around the glass 1 cm (½ in) from the top on one side to the same distance from the stem at the bottom. Take time to adjust the band evenly for best results. The width of the band will determine the space between the coloured areas; the band measurement given is the minimum you should use. It is advisable to avoid the lip line if using a paint other than that specified.

YOU WILL NEED

Set of glasses and carafe

Jam jar for practice runs

3 x 5 mm (¼ in) rubber bands for each item to be decorated

Porcelaine 150 glass paints in your choice of opaque colours

Porcelaine 150 outliner

Small piece of fur fabric or fine sponge for each colour being used

Saucer covered in cling film to speed the cleaning up process

Scalpel

Domestic oven

VARIATIONS

Add a matching carafe to the set using a different colour in each section to unite it with the glasses. Experiment with different colour combinations and outliners. This idea can be adapted to make little candle holders decorated with solvent-based paints to give a stained glass effect.

2 Repeat with the second and third rubber bands aiming to spread them equally around the bowl of the glass so that all the sections to be painted are roughly the same size. If you are planning to decorate a carafe to match the set, add bands to it as well.

3 Pour a little paint into the saucer and then sponge the spaces between the bands with your chosen colour. Apply the colour lightly and evenly for best results. We painted all six areas the same colour on each glass but you could use six different colours. Paint the stems too, as we have, or leave them plain. Leave for 24 hours to dry before being tempted to go on to step 4!

4 Remove the bands and you will find that the paint has seeped under the rubber where they cross. Use a scalpel to neaten up the edges.

5 Using the outliner, apply tiny dots around each block of colour to give a really neat finish. Remember that the outliner tends to spread slightly so leave space between each dot. (It might be worth practising first on a jam jar.) If you are happy with the result, leave for a further 24 hours before baking following manufacturer's instructions. If not, wash the design off and start again! Wash the glasses before use.

FROSTED GLASS WINDOW

Here is a cheap but attractive alternative to frosted glass. It is also a good substitute for net curtaining at windows where you need a little extra privacy. The painting may be done on the inside of an existing window if self-curing paint is used, or on a sheet of glass cut to size as we have done, in which case oven-bake paints may be used for scratch resistance. Use a photocopier to enlarge or reduce the pattern to suit any size of window.

1 Enlarge the pattern using a photocopier to the size required if necessary. Use aerosol mount to attach it to the thin card (if using). Leave to dry for at least ten minutes before cutting the stencil. Place the pattern onto the cutting mat and use the scalpel to cut out the design carefully. Keep the cockerel for step 3.

YOU WILL NEED

A piece of glass (ours is 22 cm (8½ in) square)	Opaque white glass paint such as Vitrail or Porcelaine 150 matt medium
Template (page 73)	Paintbrushes
A sheet of paper or card the same size as the glass if you wish to reuse the template	Water or white spirit, depending upon paint used
Scalpel with a no 11 blade or craft knife	Saucer covered with cling film to make the cleaning up process easier!
Cutting mat or thick newspaper to protect the worksurface	Scrap of fine sponge or fur fabric
Aerosol adhesive mount	Typist's rubber or halved cocktail stick (toothpick) for etching
Glass cleaner or warm, soapy water	Cotton bud
Old leather gloves for handling the glass	Domestic oven
Offcut of coloured fabric or paper	

VARIATIONS

If you omit the cockerel, this design would look good as a frame for a mirror. With the addition of a few more squares, the pattern can easily be elongated and a row of cockerels added!

2 Thoroughly clean the glass with warm soapy water or glass cleaner and make sure it is completely dry before sponging. Lay the glass onto a piece of coloured paper or fabric so that you can see what you are doing. Use a light spray of adhesive mount on the back of the stencil, leave to dry for a few seconds and then position it centrally on the glass.

3 Pour some opaque white paint into the saucer and use the sponge or fur fabric to apply the paint evenly over the outer design. Hold the glass up to the light to check for even density. Sponge the cockerel last and then remove the stencil with great care and admire before quickly moving on to the next stage!

4 Use the typist's rubber or cocktail stick to etch in the eye, wing and other details of the cockerel using the template as a guide.

5 Finally, remove any stray paint which has managed to work its way under the stencil using a cotton bud and then leave to dry for at least 24 hours. Alternatively, use a scalpel to remove the paint once it is completely dry. Bake if appropriate.

TIP

If using oven-bake paints, remember to use a
pane of glass which will fit inside the oven.

FLORAL ROUNDELS

These roundels make a refreshing change from the usual stained glass versions that are now seen everywhere. They are a perfect way to brighten up a window and look attractive when the sunlight shines through them.

1 If your roundel is not the same size as ours, use a photocopier to enlarge or reduce the template to the required dimmensions. Lay the template on the worksurface and tape the roundel over it, being careful to position the tape over plain areas of the pattern.

VARIATIONS

These designs could be used as jam pot covers if the designs were worked on cellophane using black paint instead of outliner. Enlarge or reduce the design according to the size of the jar and use white tissue underneath it to show off the design.

2 With the outliner, carefully follow the outlines of the flowers and leaves using steady, even pressure. Start at the top and work towards yourself to avoid smudging. Keep a paper towel to hand to remove any blobs of outliner from the tip of the nozzle. Leave to dry or speed up the process with the hairdryer.

3 If there are any imperfections in the outlining they can be salvaged at this stage. Use a scalpel to scratch off any rough areas and use the paintbrush to gently brush loosened outliner away from the surface.

4 Practise your brush strokes on cellophane using the ruby paint. Once you are confident, start working on the flowers and brush the petals from the centre outwards to obtain light, feathery strokes.

5 Finally, paint the leaves with the green paint varying the density of the paint for a more realistic effect and to build up depth.

TURQUOISE GALLERY

Stoppered bottle
White lilies have been painted on this bottle with silver used for the stamens. Look through flower catalogues for similar ideas.

Tall turquoise vase
Gold outliner has been applied to give a 'punched' look in simple spirals and curves.

Floral jar
Bottom: Green and silver paints were used to brighten up this jam jar. A little white was added to the silver for the outer parts of the petals and the white dots of paint applied last.

Goldfish jar
Below: This would be fun to fill with bubble bath as a gift for a child. The fish were painted with outliner first and then with a coat of clear yellow glass paint.

Fish platter
Gold was lightly brushed on the back of this plate and then a variety of blues, greens and turquoises painted over it.

Two-tone glass

Bottom: Transparent oven-bake paints in green and blue were sponged onto this little glass to give a graduated effect.

Multi-faceted jug

This old jug was picked up at a junk shop and transformed by being sponged with a range of oven-bake paints. Pewter outliner was then dotted around each colour.

Marbled plate

The edge of the plate was painted with gold and allowed to dry before turquoise, green, purple and gold paints were floated on water, and the plate marbled with them.

Cup and saucer

Below: Just imagine sipping fruit tea from this cup, beautifully painted with blackcurrants. Why not make a set featuring a variety of fruits?

Tall vase

Simple brushstrokes in shades of blues, greens and gold make this a very quick and easy project.

Turquoise tumbler

Left: The black lines were applied first and then green, white and gold paints to fill some of the spaces.

Clip frame

Black outliner was allowed to trail in wiggly lines around the frame. Once it was dry, some of the spaces were filled with green, gold and purple paints.

Encrusted bottle

Chunky glass nuggets were first glued in place on this bottle and the design worked around them.

MARBLED PLATE

Decorate the back of a glass plate with this attractive combination of techniques to produce designer tableware. You may be lucky enough to have one of these plain glass plates, so popular in the 1960s, at the back of your cupboard. If not, they are still readily available in department stores.

1 Run the tape around the plate about 5 mm (¼ in) from the edge and then use this as a guide to paint the silver rim. If you have a steady hand you will be able to do this freehand. Leave to dry thoroughly before removing the tape.

YOU WILL NEED

Glass plate	Water or a very thin solution of wallpaper paste
Sticky tape	
Silver solvent-based paint	Pipette
Paintbrush	Solvent-based paints in purple and yellow or colours of your choice
Silver outliner	
A bowl at least 7.5 cm (3 in) larger diameter than the plate	White spirit
	Newspapers
Plastic carrier bag or non-PVC cling film (optional)	Cellophane for practice runs
	Kitchen paper towels

TIPS

Before you begin the marbling, cover the worksurface with plenty of protective paper. Line the bowl with a polythene bag, if you wish, and fill with water to within 2.5 cm (1 in) of the top. We found that this makes the cleaning up process very easy! Be warned, however, that lining the bowl with PVC cling film and certain plastics can prevent the colours from spreading. We learnt the hard way and experimentation is essential.

Instead of using cellophane or paper to clean the surface of the water (see step 5), use a jar or small bottle to pick up the paint. You might end up with a really interesting piece!

2 The fine silver detailing is added at this stage using the outliner. Once the paint has been 'anchored' on to the rim of the plate at one side, the tube is lifted up into the air and the paint allowed to flow backwards and forwards across the plate in fluid lines. Occasionally it may break but do not worry too much – it all adds to the character of the design! Allow to dry.

3 Drop the purple paint onto the surface of the water or wallpaper paste using a pipette or cocktail stick and it will spread immediately. About 5 drops will be enough. For best results, speed is of the essence now.

4 Using the pipette, add a few drops of the second colour and then use the cocktail stick to swirl the colours gently into a pleasing pattern.

5 If you are not happy with the pattern you have created, remove it by lifting it off the surface using cellophane or paper towels and start again. When you are pleased with the result, pick up the plate at the very edges, position it over the marbled pattern and then tip it towards you slightly and down onto the marbled surface. Carefully rock the plate away from you so that it picks up the pattern on the surface of the watery solution. Turn it upside down and stand it on a small tin or similar item. Use brush cleaner on a paper towel to remove any paint which has found its way onto the front of the plate and then leave it to dry for 24 hours.

TIP

Store marbled plates with sheets of silicone paper between them to protect the pattern. The plate can be washed as long as it is not immersed in water which will damage the marbling. As there is no paint on the cutting surface, it is ideal for occasional use.

GRAPEVINE CLIP FRAME

This pretty clip frame couldn't be simpler! If you wish, you could substitute strawberries, cherries or pendulous blossoms such as wisteria or laburnum for the grapes, all depending upon your artistic ability. Use a botanical encyclopaedia for inspiration.

1 Remove the glass from the clip frame and use the cleaner to thoroughly clean both sides. Lay the glass over the template and paint all the grapes with the purple paint.

TIP

You could use a mount to mask off an oval or oblong shape. Or how about tearing the aperture from watercolour paper, roughly following the outline of the grapes?

2 Mix the chartreuse with a little yellow and paint about half the leaves with a solid colour before moving on to step 3. (Test the colour first on a piece of cellophane to check you are happy with it.)

3 Once you have painted half the leaves, use the cocktail stick (toothpick) to etch in the veins. Clean the point between etching each leaf with a paper towel. If the weather is very hot, only paint a few leaves before etching.

4 Pour some of the emerald paint into the saucer and then dip the sponge into it. Wipe any excess off on the edge of the saucer and then test the density of the sponging on a jam jar or cellophane before starting on your frame. Once you have mastered the density required, work on the frame, filling in the background with the sponging.

5 Finally, use the cocktail stick once more, this time to engrave tendrils in the sponged background. Etch around the leaves too if the background is very dense behind them. Once you are pleased with the result, leave it in a safe place to dry for 24 hours before assembling it.

PASTA JAR

Brighten up your pasta jar with these colourful Italian flags. This project is perfect for a beginner as no artistic ability is required! Tie a large bow around it and fill with spaghetti for an attractive inexpensive present.

1 Wash the pasta jar thoroughly in warm, soapy water and dry thoroughly. Cut the greaseproof paper to fit around the jar and cut off about 5 mm (¼ in) down one side. Stick the paper lightly to the jar. Stick the string to the top of the jar and then wind it around and around the jar before taping the string in place at the bottom of the jar. Aim for about three rotations. Using the string as a guide, draw a continuous line onto the paper.

YOU WILL NEED

Pasta jar
Tracing or greaseproof paper
Scissors
String
Sticky tape
Pen
Ruler
Flag patterns (page 76)
Black pen
Enough pasta to fill the jar
Opaque glass paint such as Ceramic à L'Eau in black, red, green, blue and white
No 2 paintbrush
Hairdryer (optional)
Water
Domestic oven

2 Remove the string and lay the paper flat. Place the flags equally on the line by measuring even gaps between them. Use the five variations of flags given and draw them along the line. You now have a pattern which will fit snugly into your pasta jar.

3 Place the pattern into the jar and fill it with pasta to hold it in place. Paint the line with the black paint using either a straight line or a rope pattern if you are more adventurous, but experiment first on a piece of cellophane. Use the hairdryer to speed the process if you are impatient.

4 Paint the green section on each flag next, again allowing the colour to dry before moving on. If necessary, mix a little blue with the green to achieve the correct shade.

5 Change the water and clean your paintbrush very well before painting the white part of each flag. Allow it to dry and then finish with the red and leave for 24 hours to dry before baking following the manufacturer's instructions.

TEXTURED FRUIT TUMBLERS

There is no need for a template when the design is embossed in the glass as it is in these tumblers. This makes it ideal as a beginner's project. The tumblers are made from recycled glass and similar glassware is widely available. Use the idea on embossed jugs and wine bottles too, and choose jewel-like colours to produce a luscious look.

1 Thoroughly wash and dry the glasses in hot soapy water to remove any trace of grease and then dry them in a cool oven. Choose the colours you want to use and test them on a sheet of cellophane before starting on the glassware. Start by painting the lemons and orange slices with the yellow paint.

YOU WILL NEED

| Embossed glasses |
| Porcelaine 150 glass paints in orange, pink, purple, yellow and green |
| Cellophane |
| No 2 paintbrush |
| Water |
| Kitchen paper towels |
| Domestic oven |

─── TIP ───

You can easily unite a collection of mismatched textured glassware by painting it in the same colours.

2 Using the orange paint, highlight the citrus slices to give them depth and a rich, fruity look. You may wish to build up colours by using two or more coats of paint.

3 We have chosen a cerise pink for these cherries but if you prefer a brighter look, use a strong red or even a really dark mix of purple and red paint to imitate juicy black cherries.

4 The grapes are painted using the purple. Do not worry if the paint does not lie flat on the surface of the grapes as the nature of the paint is such that it has an uneven effect. In this project this is of benefit as it reflects the natural bloom of the fruit.

5 Finally, paint the foliage green. Leave the tumblers to dry for 24 hours and then bake according to manufacturer's instructions. Wash the glasses before use.

RED GALLERY

Sundae dish

Below: The top part of the dish was sponged with red, while gold was used for the lower part. Once dry, tiny spots of gold outliner were added as a decorative pattern.

Fleur de lys jar

Bottom left: Flat-sided jam jars are ideal for decorating. This one was sponged first and then the design added with gold outliner.

Triangular red bottle

Bottom: Sponging forms the basis of the pattern on both these bottles. Outliner has been used for the relief patterns.

Valentine platter

Simple and sweet for the one you love!

Faceted jar

This design was inspired by old glassware and could be used very effectively in a range of colours on a set of sundae dishes or tumblers.

Octagonal dish

Positive and negative stencilling has been used to decorate this dish with heart motifs.

Heart-shaped crown bottle

Bottom: Coloured glass bottles are widely available and are easy to decorate. This one features simple but effective designs.

Bow glass

The bottom part of this glass was sponged with gold. Once dry, the bow motif was stencilled on. You could cut your own stencil or use a commercial one.

Strawberry cup

Bottom: You do need some artistic skill to reproduce this design, but it could be simplified or even stencilled. Why not paint a set of glass cups with a selection of fruits and use them to serve fruit teas?

Faceted jug

This wonderful old jug was found at a local junk shop. It lends itself to this kind of decoration and similar pieces of glass are easy to find. A combination of painting and relief work has been used.

Spotty bottle

Mineral drinks come in a superb range of shapes and sizes and are ideal for revamping and re-using.

CHRISTMAS PLATTER

It seems a pity to cover the design on this Christmas plate but it is perfect for serving up hot mince pies on a wintry day. The pattern is on the back, making a series of these plates ideal as special dinner plates if they are washed with care. Christmas trees or ivy leaves could be substituted for holly.

1 Make the reverse stencil for the gold edging by folding a piece of paper in half and then into quarters. Fold in half diagonally twice so that you have 16 layers of paper with the fold lines radiating out from the central point. Use the ruler to measure the radius of the flat base of the plate, and then mark this measurement on the paper from the central point outwards. Cut the 'V' shape as shown in the photograph. Open out the paper (you should have a circle with a pointed edge) and lightly spray with aerosol mount. Leave for a few seconds and then stick to the back of the plate.

YOU WILL NEED

Glass plate — ours is 25 cm (10 in) in diameter
Ruler
Paper
Pen or pencil
Scissors
Scalpel with no 11 blade
Cutting mat
Holly leaf and star patterns (page 76)
Aerosol adhesive spray mount
Solvent-based glass paints in gold, red and green (we mixed emerald and chartreuse for the holly)
Fine sponge or fur fabric
No 2 paintbrush

VARIATIONS

Why not make a complete set of Christmas glasses to match the plate? The holly design could be reduced on a photocopier and the holly and berries painted around the glass bowl. Sponge gold on the base, stem and bottom of the bowl.

2 Pour a little of the gold paint into the saucer and then sponge over the edge of the template all the way round. Apply the paint densely at the edge of the template to give a sharp outline and less densely near the rim of the plate. Remove the template and leave to dry.

3 Meanwhile, cut the holly stencils using the holly patterns given on page 76. As the points of the leaves are very fine, it is worth using a new scalpel blade before attempting to cut them. Cut out the stars too. Use a cutting mat to protect the worksurface and leave a border of about 1 cm (½ in) around each one. Lightly spray the backs with the aerosol adhesive.

4 Stencil the gold stars in the centre and allow them to dry. Mix the green paints to achieve the desired colour and then stencil about three leaves around the base of the plate using the sponge. Use the photo as a guide and vary the angle of the leaves as you go. We have given you three different leaf sizes to make it look more interesting. Use the cocktail stick to etch in the veining details of each leaf before stencilling the next three.

5 Use the paintbrush to fill in the gaps with the holly berries. We have mixed a rich ruby red colour for them. Leave to dry thoroughly before using.

TEMPLATES

The templates shown here are actual size.
They may be easily enlarged or reduced on a
photocopier to suit the size of the glass to
be decorated.

Goldfish plate
Large and small fish,
centre fish and wave motif
(see page 18)

Olive oil bottle
Olive spray (see page 20)

Ruby and gold sundae dishes
Leaf and tendril design (see page 28)

Millefiori lantern
(see page 26)

Tasselled champagne glasses
Rope and tassels (see page 38)

Fifties-style carafe and tumblers
Six different motifs (see page 34)

71

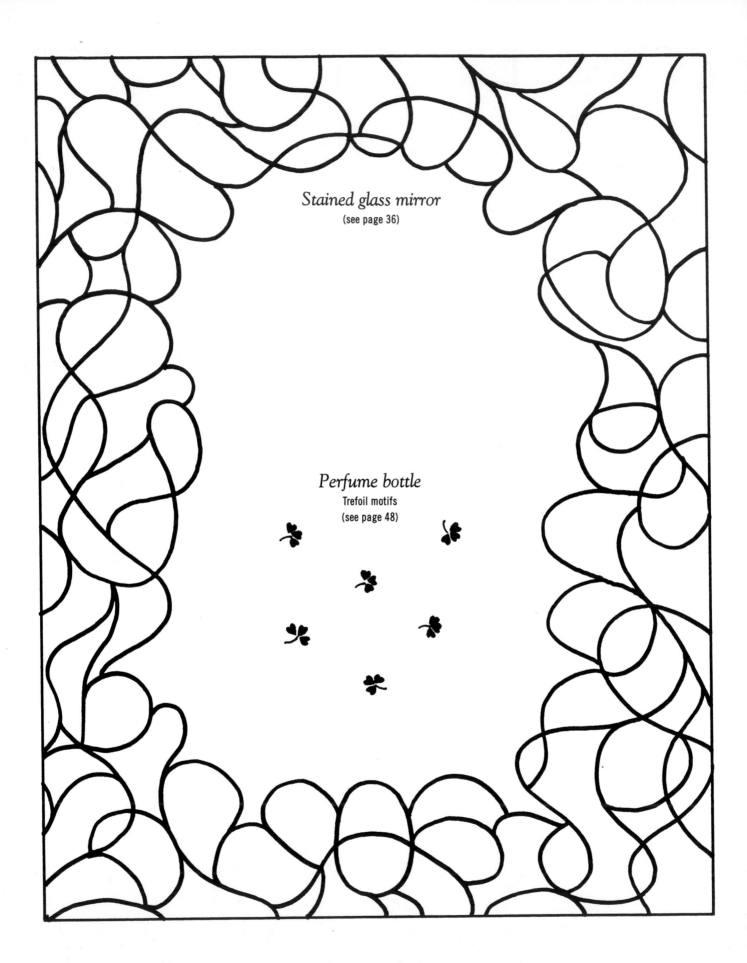

Stained glass mirror
(see page 36)

Perfume bottle
Trefoil motifs
(see page 48)

Frosted glass window
Cockerel, heart and blocks pattern
for stencil making
(see page 52)

Starry oil burner
Star shapes (see page 44)

Floral roundels
(see page 54)

Grapevine clip frame
(see page 60)

Pasta jar (see page 62)

Christmas platter (see page 68)

Practice patterns for getting started (see page 9)

Floral border
(Used on book cover – repeat
the design for each corner
using both sides of the tracing)

Getting started heart stencil design
(see page 12)

SUPPLIERS

UNITED KINGDOM

Fred Aldous
P.O. Box 135
37 Lever Street
Manchester
M1 1LW
Tel: (0161) 236 2477
Fax: (0161) 236 6075
(*Suppliers of a wide range of craft products. Mail order*)

Clearcraft
Units 16, 19 & 20
Kingston Farm
Downhall Road
Matching, Harlow
Essex CM17 0RB
Tel: (01279) 732360
Online:
www.clearcraftltd.co.uk
(*Oil burners shown on page 24, 44*)

Egyptian House
77 Wigmore Street
London
W1H 9NJ
Tel: (020) 7935 9839
and
61 Knightsbridge
London
SW1X 7RA
Tel: (020) 7235 1411
(*Coloured glassware*)

Emmaus UK
48 Kingston Street
Cambridge
CB1 2NU
Tel: (01223) 576103
(*Second-hand glassware*)

Panduro Hobby
Westway House
Transport Avenue
Brentford
Middlesex
TW8 9HF
Tel: (020) 8847 6161
(*Suppliers of Pébéo paints. Mail order*)

Philip & Tacey Ltd
North Way
Andover
Hampshire
SP10 5BA
Tel: (01264) 332171
(*Suppliers of Pébéo glass paints, including Porcelaine 150 and Vitrail. Telephone for your nearest stockist*)

Homecrafts Direct
P.O. Box 38
Leicester
LE1 9BU
Tel: (0845) 458 4531
Fax: (0845) 458 4532
Online:
www.homecrafts.co.uk
(*Mail order suppliers of a wide range of craft products*)

SOUTH AFRICA

Art Leather and
Handcraft
Shop 107
Musgrave Centre
124 Musgrave Road
Durban
Tel: (031) 21 9517

Corner Arts and Crafts
52 4th Avenue
Newton Park
Port Elizabeth
Tel: (0431) 57 231

Cottage Craft
20 Pearce Street
East London
Tel: (0431) 57 231

The Craftsman
Shop 10
Progress House
Bordeaux Drive
Randburg
Tel: (011) 886 0441

Crafty Supplies
32 Main Road
Claremeont
Cape Town
Tel: (021) 61 0286

Mycrafts Shop
Aliwal Street
Bloemfontein
Tel: (051) 48 4119

AUSTRALIA

Elde Crafts
76 Main Street
Hahndorf
South Australia
Tel: (08) 388 7007

Oxford Art Supplies
221-223 Oxford Street
Darlinghurst
NSW 2010
Tel: (02) 360 4066

Boronia Arts & Crafts
Centre
247 Dorset Road
Boronia
Victoria 3155
Tel: (03) 762 1751

Sundale Handcrafts
Shop 11
Logan Hyperdome
Pacific Highway
Loganholme
Queensland 4129
Tel: (07) 801 1121

Arts & Crafts Corner
34 Mint Street
East Victoria Park
Western Australia
6101
Tel: (09) 361 4567

NEW ZEALAND

Auckland Folk Art
Centre
591 Remuera Road
Upland Village
Auckland
Tel: (09) 524 0936

Dominion Paint
Centre
227 Dominion Road
Mt Eden
Tel: (09) 638 7593

P A Inkman Ltd
36 Douglas Street
Ponsonby
Auckland
Tel: (09) 638 7593

Studio Art Supplies
225 Parnell Road
Parnell
Auckland
Tel: (09) 377 0302

ACKNOWLEDGEMENTS

The authors and publishers would like to say a very big thank you to Pébéo, in particular John Wright of Pébéo UK and Carol Hook from Clear Communications Ltd, who have been so generous in their supply of paints, especially Porcelaine 150 and Vitrail, which we have used almost exclusively in this book.

Thank you to Clearcraft for their beautiful glass oil burners and to the Egyptian House who generously supplied us with a selection of their lovely coloured and recycled glass. Thanks to Shona for her patience, stamina and superb photographs and to Yvonne for letting us write this book! Thank you to the Cambridge branch of Emmaus, the self-help group for the homeless, for having such an abundance of glassware at incredibly good prices just crying out to be painted (we hope there is a branch near you).

INDEX